Gone Back To Get It

A Slim Collection of Rememories

Tasha Gomes

India | USA | UK

Copyright © Tasha Gomes
All Rights Reserved.

This book has been self-published with all reasonable efforts taken to make the material error-free by the author. No part of this book shall be used, reproduced in any manner whatsoever without written permission from the author, except in the case of brief quotations embodied in critical articles and reviews.

The Author of this book is solely responsible and liable for its content including but not limited to the views, representations, descriptions, statements, information, opinions, and references ["Content"]. The Content of this book shall not constitute or be construed or deemed to reflect the opinion or expression of the Publisher or Editor. Neither the Publisher nor Editor endorse or approve the Content of this book or guarantee the reliability, accuracy, or completeness of the Content published herein and do not make any representations or warranties of any kind, express or implied, including but not limited to the implied warranties of merchantability, fitness for a particular purpose.

The Publisher and Editor shall not be liable whatsoever...

Made with ❤ on the BookLeaf Publishing Platform
www.bookleafpub.in
www.bookleafpub.com

Dedication

This collection of Rememory is dedicated to my children: Ylaysia, Isaiah, Antonio and Analisa.
May your ears be attuned to the true story of You.

I love you.

To my ancestors, blood and kindred. May these words honor You and give rise to your voices. May my hands be used as lightning rods.

I love you.

And I hope that you too, Reader, soon find yourself in the embrace of your own Rememory.

I love you.

Preface

This collection is an exploration of one soul's memories, some of the lessons and some of the threads that shape an achingly beautiful Life. It is a conversation of sorts, sometimes between the narrator and the reader, at times between the narrator's conscious and unconscious bodies, and at times between the narrator and a memory.

Each of these poems is based on a specific moment, a memory being *re*visited, *re*imagined, *re*told. Each poem is a *re*memory. A creative retelling of the past, with the hope of informing the future. The structure of the poems may vary, but what they share is this: each poem is written to be read aloud. The lines and stanzas are structured to be read as they should be heard; try reading any of these poems aloud, pause where punctuation suggests, **and** take a quick inhale at the end of each line. The poem's rhythm and cadence will be revealed in those breaths and pauses.

The book's title, *Gone Back to Get It*, is a call back to the spirit of Sankofa, which can be translated as "go back and get it." Sankofa suggests that to prosper in the future, we must look to the lessons of our history. The title suggests that the narrator has indeed, gone back to get those lessons; and here they are, in this slim collection of poems.

Acknowledgements

I would like to express gratitude for my sister, Nesha. For her never ending support, for the moments she hyped me to the moon and back, at times aggressively so.

I would be remiss to miss an opportunity to acknowledge the gifts of our shared ancestor, Toni Morrison. My vision was forever changed by *The Bluest Eye*. Toni gave us wings.

1. Water

i remember.
i remember, yes.
how the wave of Rememory
washed me over,
flooded every empty space,
drowning out doubt until again I knew:
you are me. and i am you. for

i do.
cry oceans and bleed rain.
sip sweat and pour hurricanes.

i do.
see Self in waterspouts and placid lakes.
hear my tummy rumble in your thunder.
feel my pulse find rhythm in your waves.

i know.
we carry the same destructive potential.
our medicine must be, and is, torrential.
and

i am.
in your surface reflecting Light.

i am.
in your bubbles fostering Life.

i am.
in the cascades carving new routes

i am.
in the soil of my ancestors, strengthening roots.

i am.
baptized in your Rememory.
and you
in mine.

2. may i ask

i want to ask
when you knew.
[that it was time to go.]
how did you know?

who opened the door for you and
why did it take so long?

may i ask,
how i'll know
when the road is longer than it need be,
when the climb is too much for tired knees
when the dives too far and far too deep,
the price to carry on,
simply. too. steep.

may i ask,
how will i know
when i have arrived?
who will open the door for me
and why do they take so long?

may i ask
how i am supposed to remember tomorrow

and look forward to yesterday, while
holding all of the Rememories,
and none of the cards.

3. Fear

fear.

fear is a dastardly thing.
a bastardly thing.
fear spends its quiet hours sharpening teeth, filing claws,
perfecting aim, listening for the invite.
fear lies low and silent, only moving to strike. StrikE.
STRIKE.
quickly. accurately. pointedly. devastatingly.
camouflaged and covert, until. UNTIL,
you realize you didn't see it coming. or going.
without knowing, you
just yelped, gnashed, lashed, cried out at
the wound, which appeared so suddenly that
the only thing to blame was He who stood before you,
HE, who bears no culpability,
yet shoulders the blame owed to
the dastardly
bastardly
Thing that lies
behind your blazing eyes,
your wringing hands, with
sharpened teeth, greedy tongue. fueled,
by your pain. fed,

by the mystery. never satiated, but
woefully encouraged, because

one
broken thing
has become

two.

4. elipses

it's just that,
your love of ellipses suggested...

an invitation ... to an alternative ending. maybe a

continuation... or

speculation ... perhaps

ambiguity . . . and

an absence of Resolution .. . with

open interpretation . . . promises of

continued conversation .. . but

until then ... we Believe.

5. slowly the tongue moves

i opened my mouth
to say those three words, but

too slowly the tongue moves.

Fear jumped the line and
changed the order of Things and
rearranged the top and the bottom and
only shadows were released.

Woman.

if you are tortured, it is
because you are the co-conspirer.

you moved your tongue too slow and
left space for the bastardly Thing to
crowdoutthetruth and
smother the light that
should fill the space between you
and your reflection.

2. night flight

it starts with this scene:

he: *do you know what today is?*

she: *it is the day we venture to Somewhere New!*
[eyes beaming with clouds and starburst and mist]

he: *that it is. grab your things, but*
only the things you need, to
fuel our trip and unfold when we land.
[rocking from heel to toe, he beams like a wand in the sand]

when the moon was high and
the sky was bright,
without the threat of too-strong sunlight,
they walked hand in hand,
heart in heart,
aboard the winged catamaran.

she - with pockets full of chews and
heart full of thumps, and
he - with head full of plans
and chest full of jumps.

he: *take your place my dear.*
[and indeed she did, just behind the sail,
as he moved in position to steer.]

he: *in Somewhere New, there are waterfalls, and
they fly over mossy stones, and they
slide through the lushest gullies, and they
whisper and they roar.*

she: [took a deep inhale and
blew all of her faith into the sail.
and off they soar.]

he: *in Somewhere New, there are mountains that
hold whole villages and
temples and
parties and ...
Hope.*

she: [with eyes closed, inhaled more truth
and a sailful of Rememory she blew.]

he: *in Somewhere New, there are
castles by the sea, with
flags of sugar and
moats filled with cream.*

she: breathed in hope until
her belly was full of Rememory, and then
she puckered her lips to fill the sail, and
the catamaran sped
through cloud whisps and
over sleeping jungles and
between moonrays and starshine, and
into the realm of Somewhere New. where

Rememory is currency and fuel. and
hope and belief sustain life. and
love is spoken with fluency. and
Nirvana can be reached by kite.

7. ancestors

remember that time you
knew you couldn't, but
did It anyway.

did you think you were alone?

when the crowd said "no"
and history said "no"
and your skeletons whispered,
so you hesitated by the door.

did you *really* think it was *you* alone,
who shouldered that world?

when the sky opened arms
and the river whispered psalms
and the earth softened,
just enough
to offer you footing to
leave your imprint as evidence
that you,
had moved on.

when wind came through to clear the path

and the fire in you burned fear to ash,
and those who walked before you sighed
victory chants.
silent mantras.
forbidden songs,
resurrected from invisibility.

it was Those Who Walked Before You
who cried
joyful rivers, and
mournful pools, and
vengeful typhoons, until

you, arrived.

welcome,
they sang.
finally,
they praised. for

they knew.
they knew you.
they knew you could.
they knew you would.

8. hoodoo

vodou
hoodoo
i do
you do
she do
we do
vodou
hoodoo.

did you wince,
when you heard those syllables?

did you gasp? when you saw
your mama's saints, all
dressed in white, and
shaded black, and
offered the sweetest
libations.

were you outraged? when they
accepted your rosary, then
made it sing, and
learned to ring
your bells,

but better?

fear not.
we are kin.
for

i do
you do
she do
we do,
saints do

hoodoo too.

9. one drop

that's all it takes.

this i learned the hardest of ways.
when day went night.
pizza burger, ruined.
and everything tasted of cotton.

dance, interrupted.
masks, removed.
scene, cut.
rude.

all it took was that one drop.
that once hardly visible,
now inescapable,
then sweet caramel
now pathogenic, and
downright *offensive*...

all it took was a drop.

to make everything feel of cotton.
words, choking on suffocating tufts.
words, hardly heard through ears now muffed.

words, unseen for the thorn-drawn red.
words, landing softly on my boll of a head.
so,

what a difference a drop makes.
(by the way) it was mother's fault.
she ruined the harvest
without a single thought, so
here i am:
cotton-stuffed and silent,
ginned and drowning
in that single,
cursed,
drop.

10. frivolity

frivolity.
the urgency of frivolity.

as resistance and gratitude.
as resilience and fortitude.
as audacity and tenacity.
and the bravery
and the beauty in being YOU.
there is a beautiful rage in that tutu.

your strength is fomented in your frivolity.

your twirl says, "I'm still here. I'm still Me. and I'm still free."

11. what you are

in times of darkness,
remember this.
you are the carrier of hopes and dreams
and 'dare not believes.'

you are the inheritor of
wind
water
earth
and fire.

you are the harvest, fed by
tears
sweat
ache
and ire.

it is no surprise that
there is heat in your chest.
mud between your toes.
groundswell behind your eyes.
exhalations in tornadoes.

you have no choice, but to

carry lightning bolts in knotted fists
and sound thunder in every step, as you
part seas and bring down
sheets of scouring water
and boiling revenge,
for you were formed in the image of THOSE gods
who turn scythe to Wild and slay the beasts to
blaze the trail,
for those who will walk behind you.

12. we were mermaids

before the reckoning,
before the deciders decided
that in order to be truly civilized we must
wear shoes,
we were mermaids.
and we were free.

the problem with mermaid
an**a**-toe-mee
is that mermaids weren't meant
to have feet, you see.

so. in order to fit
the new order of things
the mermaid acquiesced and
clipped her sea wings.

so. sea flight was shelved, as
plank walking commenced.

and. coral grazing ceased, and
kitchen toiling reigned best.

and. warriors' tools were stripped,

and land bodies were primped.

and. every effort was given
to make us forget,
that before we were the rib,
we were mermaids.
too powerful to be pimped.

but you.
you remember.
and that is the root of your problems, my dear.
you yearn for the time of sea wings and coral
while admiring your shoes in the mirror.

13. the gift

give a man a fish and
he'll kidnap the giver.
and the fish.

bite the hand that feeds him.
march the giver to the bank
and pillage the river too.

strip the fish of its name
and ceremoniously lay claim
to the whole entire species,
then call the giver insane.

drown the protests with fire,
throw rocks and hide his hand,
play victim, draw ire
blame the stewards of the land.

flag in the air,
finger on the trigger,
eyes wild as violence,
driven to make his catch bigger.

when you give a man a fish

please please do beware,
that man might take your fish
then lay your land bare.

14. shouldering

feet get heavy,
a side effect of living.

mind gets muddy,
a side effect of knowing.

hands get chaffed,
knees get scuffed,
eyes get milked,
wrists get cuffed,
throat gets stuffed
cries get cut
but we dance on
cause we
are tough.

by assignment. but.
beneath the lacquer

heart gets full,
a side effect of loving.

gaze gets soft,
a side effect of hoping.

fingers mingle,
eyes twinkle,
hums escape,
dreams break
away from night prisons
and broken systems
to carry us across watas
and through tree lines, and
straight into the heart of our auntie's hearth
and onto the grounds of our baba's earth
where never before has a soul heard the words
that transformed us from royalty to despot.

15. raven knows your name

doubt will creep up behind you on this road.
your first thought may be to quicken your step,
clutch your sweater a little tighter at the throat.

you may start to bow before you know it,
a slight hunch curving you into humility,
bending your back in such a way that your
gaze doesn't raise above the ground.

doubt will glide, silent but dogged in his pursuit,
leading with a crooked and accusatory finger,
closing the gap cause
you slowed to listen to what's not being said.

in these moments, when doubt is aiming
and you are shrinking
and there is not enough room between you and the pestilence,
you will feel the need to end your journey and crouch in the path.

i urge you to recall that the raven knows your name.
that winds are delighted to greet you in the forest, and
sun comes down to kiss your face, and

you breathe out tornadoes, and
laugh in thunder,
and build entire worlds.
and raven knows your name.

there is no shadow dark enough to smother your light.

16. djembe

i have a beautiful drum.
it used to belong to a lover of mine.
in the end he was trash,
but this drum?
this drum is divine.

it is worn from hands
that speak in staccato.

this drum opens portals.
don't believe?

agoo

17. by the creek

i visited our creek today
and poured all of my regrets
into her white water.

i told her about the times
i should have held my daughter,
the days i yelled when
i should have been softer,
the mornings i rushed,
so much that i didn't see
that my son was looking beyond me
and days had become assembly lines
and nights couldn't come fast enough, but
i tried...

creek just bubbled.

18. woman math

just try to build a woman today.
the math is nearly impossible.

they're either
too thin or too thick.
so you take an inch from here to
add an ounce there.
divide the thighs,
and cat the eyes.
you plump the rump,
snatch the waist,
stuff in pumps,
and lift the face.
and then the algorithm changes
now your math is out of date.

so just what *is* the circumference
of the ideal waist?

and can we get to the square root of this sew in,
and triple her eyelash length?

and double the drugs.

she needs to be numb
if you want to avoid a fuss.

19. beauty

there's so much beauty left in the world.
i know it's hard to believe
when everywhere the messaging
is saying something different.

there's so much beauty living in this world.
and if it's hard to see,
you're probably moving way too fast,
tracking screens instead of bees.

beauty calls us to pause in dusk's soft light
to smile at chirpers serenading the night.

beauty wafts on breezes
and speckles falling leaves.
beauty spirals gardenia's flowers
and makes majesty out of oak trees.

beauty dances on water
and turns fireflies on,
adds glitter to sun rays
and skyviews to ponds.

beauty glides on silent wings

against kaleidoscope skies.

it is everything i see in you
when you open your eyes.

21. emigration

what if ...

we packed a boat with all of them
and set it out to sea,

for a transatlantic party
to manifest their destiny.

we'll bring the kids down to the shore
to bid the crew adieux!

we'll have balloons, a banjo
and some fireworks too.

[the legal kind.]

22. shape shifter

sometimes i am a volcano.
sometimes, i well up and become a volcano
when it's time to burn bridges and change the landscape.

sometimes i am a dragon.
i am a dragon when i need wings,
an educator when i clock in,
and a black girl twenty-four-seven.

i am a daughter, four times over,
bidding her fading father good bye.

i am a mother,
raising beautiful black boys to fly.

i can do all that.
and though this is not an exhaustive list,
it is becoming an exhausting task.

shape shifting is a natural consequence
and in fact became necessity,
dropping one toe in front of the other,
crossing wires i couldn't see.
doing my best with every step to keep

the wind at my back and the sun in my face.

at times i found myself bending to the wind,
becoming smaller, turning
to face a new direction altogether,
somehow becoming lighter and taller.
always adapting to changing conditions
in order to keep it moving.

we've twisted too much.

and now i stand.
a cooling volcano,
welcoming a calm sky,
with hissing tantrums of yesterday
still ringing in my ears.

i am content to lie here,
sky facing, open mouthed,
unmoved by the magma pulling
and pushing in these veins,
welcoming the stone storms i can't avoid.
today, under my hood,
i'm still shape shifting. but slowly.
intentionally, and comfortably.
i am settling into my place on this earth.

i am becoming a mountain.

www.ingramcontent.com/pod-product-compliance
Lightning Source LLC
Chambersburg PA
CBHW070040070426
42449CB00012BA/3116